STUDENT COOKBOOK

Written by Nat Lambert

imagine THAT!™

Imagine That! is an imprint of Top That! Publishing plc,
Tide Mill Way, Woodbridge, Suffolk, IP12 1AP, UK
www.topthatpublishing.com
Copyright © 2010 Top That! Publishing plc
Imagine That! is a trademark of Top That! Publishing plc.

GW00420203

Contents

Contents

Desserts

Smoothies

Your Own Recipes

Introduction

Okay, so you've left home for the first time and Mum's not around to do the cooking. Where do you begin? Whether you're living on your own, in a shared house or in halls of residence, this book is designed to help you take that first step into the daunting world of cooking and make it as smooth and easy as possible – remember, it's not as scary as it sounds!

This book will not only introduce you to the pleasure of cooking, but also provide a basic view into the kitchen, its necessary equipment and ingredients. Ranging from snacks, main meals and desserts, an essential collection of easy-to-follow recipes are included, which will fortify you and line your stomach during the best years of your life!

Healthy Eating

Getting into a routine of healthy eating is not as impossible as it sounds – it's fine to have the occasional kebab or chips every now and then, but as long as everything is in moderation, you are well on your way to a balanced and healthy diet.

One of the most important rules to follow is to try and make an effort to eat five portions of fruit and vegetables a day. Try to have a smoothie or fruit juice for breakfast, a piece of fruit with lunch, vegetables or a salad with dinner and you're more than half way there!

Eating on a Budget

It's easy to spend all of your budget on booze, but don't forget that you still have to eat! There are handy tips throughout the book, which will have you saving in no time. All it takes is a little planning and creativity and you'll soon be eating great meals on a small amount of cash.

Introduction

Equipment

Start to gather a few essentials before you start your life as a student, and you'll be set up for the rest of the year.

A set of saucepans – an absolute must – buy three if possible; small, medium and large and also invest in a frying pan and a wok.

Utensils – from cutlery and crockery to a potato masher and tin opener, many shops sell these in a pack, which also includes a wooden spoon, peeler, grater, whisk, spatula and ladle.

Set of knives – try and find a good selection that will tackle a variety of tasks, from chopping vegetables to slicing bread.

Weighing scales – not essential, but helpful for measuring ingredients if you're unsure on how much to use. A measuring jug may come in handy also.

Chopping board – it is preferable to have two – one for meat and one for vegetables, but as long as you wash it well after it's been used for each ingredient, one should suffice.

Mixing bowl – essential for marinating, mixing and whisking.

Oven-proof dish and baking tray – great for anything that you need to place in the oven, from pies, stews or pizza!

Cleaning equipment – this includes a washing-up brush, liquid, surface sprays and tea towels.

Store Cupboard Essentials

Not only are these basic ingredients handy to have in case you need to whip up something quickly, they provide the staple of many of the recipes listed in this book.

- Salt and pepper • Olive oil • Pasta • Flour
- Butter or margarine • Eggs • Bread • Milk • Onions
- Garlic • Rice • Potatoes • Dried herbs and spices
- Chopped tomatoes

Portions

The recipes in this book have been selected so they can be prepared around a student's hectic lifestyle. When a recipe states that it will serve more than one person, you can make it a house meal or freeze individual portions for later.

Note: *The temperatures and measurements given in this book are approximate. Use the same measurement conversions throughout the recipe (grams or ounces) to maintain the correct ratios.*

Health and Safety

Keeping the kitchen clean and germ-free is essential. You don't want to be giving your new housemates food poisoning in the first week! Here are a few basic rules to make sure that doesn't happen!

Buying
Only buy fresh food from sources that you trust.

Washing
Wash all food if it is to be eaten raw, even if the food is to be peeled, such as carrots and potatoes.

Your Fridge
This should stay roughly at 4°C. It is important not to overfill it as this cuts down on circulation of the cool air. Refrigerate all meat, fish, chicken, dairy products and eggs. Keep dairy products at the top of the fridge and always cover raw meat and store it on the bottom shelf where it can't touch or drip onto other foods. Try to rotate the food in your fridge and cupboards, so the oldest stuff is eaten first. Never put warm or hot food in the fridge as this will warm up the temperature inside. Wait until it reaches room temperature before refrigerating.

Raw Meat
Raw meat contains harmful bacteria that can spread very easily to anything it touches, including other foods, worktops, chopping boards, hands and knives. It's especially important to keep raw meat away from ready-to-eat foods, such as salad, fruit and bread. As these foods won't be cooked before you eat them, the bacteria that gets onto these foods won't be killed. To help stop bacteria from spreading, remember these things:

- Don't let raw meat touch other foods.

- Never prepare ready-to-eat food using a chopping board or knife that you have used to prepare raw meat, unless they have been washed thoroughly first.

- Always wash hands, knives, boards and anything else in contact with raw meat or fish with cold water first to wash off the meat juices, then with hot soapy water and scrub well. Allow items to air dry before putting away and ensure that boards stand upright with air able to circulate around them.

- Wash your cloths and tea towels regularly.

- Use an anti-bacterial spray on kitchen surfaces before and after each cooking session.

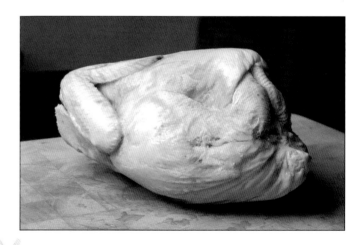

Health and Safety

Cooking

Always make sure you preheat the oven before placing food inside. Cook food as directed in the recipes to kill any bacteria that may be present.

Reheating Food

If you need to reheat food, make sure that it is hot in the centre, and when keeping food warm, make sure it is thoroughly hot first, then maintain a good holding temperature that will keep it really hot, not just lukewarm.

Freezing & Thawing

When freezing food, label and clearly mark with the date. Never refreeze thawed food without cooking it first. Thaw food overnight in the fridge, on a plate or in a plastic container in case of drips. Allow enough time for food to completely thaw.

Cooling

When cooling food for storage, try to cool it as fast as possible, so bacteria doesn't have time to grow. Never cover with a lid while cooling, as this slows things down. Never cover with cling film either as this acts just like a lid and provides warm, humid conditions that are perfect for harmful bacteria. Never leave food out overnight to cool; try to get it in the fridge within an hour of cooking.

If anything smells or looks bad, don't eat it. Food which actually looks 'off' is usually not suitable for consumption.

Keeping Neat

When you have finished cooking, make sure that preparation surfaces are free from food and the bin is taken out every day. You don't want rodents living with you too!

7

Snacks

Eggs

Eggs (fried, poached, boiled)

Eggs are so useful and versatile, from making an omelette to a boiled egg and soldiers! They should be kept in the fridge and always eaten fresh. Check the use by date on the box!

Cooking eggs

- **To fry an egg:**
  Heat a little butter in a pan until barely hot; break the egg into the pan and leave to cook gently for two minutes.

- **To poach an egg:**
  Bring a small pan of water to the boil. Add a tablespoon of vinegar (this helps to set the protein in the egg). Take an egg straight from the fridge and break it into a cup. Swirl the water in the pan with a spoon. Drop the egg into the middle, cook for one minute and turn off the heat. You may follow it with another egg as the first egg swirls round the pan. Allow the egg(s) to stand in the water for 10 minutes, then remove with a slotted spoon and allow to drain briefly on kitchen paper.

- **To cook boiled eggs:**
  Place the eggs in a pan of cold water and bring to the boil, simmering for 10 minutes for hard-boiled eggs and 4 minutes in already boiling water for a soldier-dipping yolk. Alternatively, add your eggs to a pan of boiling water, turn down the heat and simmer for 12 minutes. Place the hard boiled eggs in cold water to cool rapidly before peeling.

Student Tip
If you've just started to cook, stick to basic recipes and meals. Once you've perfected these, you can quickly move on to more complicated dishes.

Cheese Omelette

Cheese Omelette

Omelettes are quick and easy to make – perfect if you need to get out of the house quick for a lecture or a night out!

You will need:
- 2 or 3 eggs
- salt and pepper
- knob of butter
- 50 g (2 oz) cheddar cheese, grated
- parsley to garnish (optional)

Serves 1

1. Break the eggs into a bowl and season with salt and pepper. Beat with a fork until well mixed.

2. Heat a thumb-sized knob of butter in a frying pan and allow it to foam. Tip in the egg mixture and let it cover the bottom of the pan.

3. As it cooks, draw the edges into the middle with a fork. Keep going with this until the eggs are almost set, but a little creamy in the centre.

4. Remove the pan from the heat and tip the pan so that the omelette slides over to one side. Add the cheese to one side and, using a fork, fold the omelette in half. Have your plate ready and tip the omelette onto it. Garnish with parsley, if desired.

Student Tip
Scrambled egg can be made in the same way as an omelette – just stir the egg in the saucepan with a lot more vigour and do not allow the bottom to set.

Chunky Chips

Chunky Chips

These chunky wedge chips are great as a snack on their own or to serve with any number of dishes, especially a home-made burger (see page 38).

You will need:
- 4 large potatoes (1 per person)
- 4 tbsp olive oil (1 tbsp per potato)
- salt and pepper

Serves 4

1. Preheat the oven to 200°C / 400°F / gas mark 6. Wash the potatoes and cut each one into 6–8 wedges – leave the skins on.

2. Place the wedges into a bowl with an inch of water, cover with a plate, and microwave for 5–10 minutes so that a knife just penetrates the potatoes. Carefully check after 7 minutes to see how they are doing.

3. Heat the olive oil in a roasting tin and add the potatoes. Coat the potatoes in the oil and roast in the oven for 20–30 minutes, or until deep golden brown and crisp. Drain on kitchen paper and season with salt and pepper.

Student Tip
Arrange to go food shopping an hour before the store closes. Many items will be reduced and can be frozen to prolong use by dates.

Bacon, Lettuce and Tomato Sandwich

Bacon, Lettuce and Tomato Sandwich

Perfect for breakfast, lunch or dinner!

You will need:
- 25 g (1 oz) butter or margarine
- 2 slices white or brown bread
- 2 tbsp oil
- 2 rashers of bacon
- crisp leaves of lettuce
- ½ tomato, sliced
- sauce of your choice (red, brown, mayo etc.)

Serves 1

1. Spread the butter or margarine finely on both slices of bread.

2. Heat the oil in a large frying pan and add the rashers of bacon. Fry for 3–5 minutes, depending on how crispy you like it, and turn over halfway through cooking time so the rashers are cooked on both sides.

3. Meanwhile, start to layer the lettuce and sliced tomato on one slice of bread. Once the bacon has cooked, place it on top of the lettuce and tomato. Press the other slice of bread on top and squeeze down. Finish by adding a sauce of your choice, cut the sandwich in half, and enjoy.

Student Tip
Freeze bread on the day of purchase and defrost it as you need it.

Fruity Tuna Sandwich

Fruity Tuna Sandwich

This sandwich releases energy slowly – a great snack to have before a long lecture or exam!

You will need:
- 25 g (1 oz) butter or margarine
- 2 slices of brown or wholemeal bread
- ½ tin of tuna
- ½ apple, grated
- 25 g (1 oz) raisins or dried apricots
- 1 tbsp mayonnaise

Variations
- try pear instead of apple
- use cream cheese instead of mayonnaise

Serves 1

1. Spread the butter or margarine finely on both slices of bread.

2. Add the remaining ingredients to a mixing bowl, then spread onto one slice of bread.

3. Press the other slice of bread on top, squeeze down, cut the sandwich in half, and enjoy.

Student Tip
When making a recipe, prepare enough food for more than one meal and either keep it in the fridge for the next day or put it in the freezer to eat next week. Don't forget to defrost it first and reheat it thoroughly!

Cheese and Beans Toastie

Cheese and Beans Toastie

Another clear favourite in grilled sandwich recipes, this is simple, tasty, and nutritious. It's great as a quick snack at any time of the day or night.

You will need:
- 25 g (1 oz) butter or margarine
- 2 slices of white bread
- 25 g (1 oz) baked beans
- 50 g (2 oz) cheddar cheese, grated

Variations
- add some mixed herbs or barbecue sauce to the beans before cooking
- try different cheeses

Serves 1

1. Spread the butter or margarine finely on both slices and sides of the bread.

2. Spoon on the beans and sprinkle on the grated cheese.

3. Put the other slice of bread on top and place under a grill or in a toastie machine.

4. Once hot, cut in half, and enjoy.

Student Tip
Buy supermarkets' own brands – they're cheaper and often taste very similar to their more expensive counterparts.

Grilled Veggie Bruschetta

Grilled Veggie Bruschetta

A great way to some of your '5 a day'! Why not double the ingredients to make extra?

You will need:
- 1 red pepper, sliced
- 1 courgette, sliced
- 1 red onion, sliced
- 1 plum tomato, sliced
- 4 tbsp olive oil
- fresh garlic, to taste
- 2 tsp whole-grain mustard
- 4 bruschetta slices

Variations
- use whichever vegetables are in season

Serves 1

1. Place the pepper, courgette, red onion and tomato in a bowl.

2. Mix the oil, garlic and mustard in a separate bowl and then drizzle this over the vegetables.

3. Spread the vegetables on a baking tray and cook under a hot grill for 10 minutes or until browned, turning halfway.

4. Divide the vegetables between the bruschetta slices. Drizzle some oil on each one and serve.

Student Tip
If possible, buy your fresh fruit and veg from market stalls. Compare prices – they are likely to be cheaper than the supermarket.

Potato Skins

Potato Skins

Not only are they easy to make, but these cheesy skins are scrummy too!

You will need:
- 2 large potatoes
- 3 tbsp olive oil
- 4 rashers of bacon, chopped
- 1 onion, chopped
- 1 tbsp barbecue sauce (optional)
- 100 g (4 oz) cheddar cheese, grated

Makes 4

1. Preheat the oven to 200°C / 400°F / gas mark 6.

2. Scrub the large potatoes well and place them in the oven. Bake for 40–45 minutes until they feel slightly soft when squeezed. Leave to cool for a little while.

3. When cool, cut each potato in half. Scoop the inside out with a spoon (reserving for later), and leave a small layer of potato on the skin.

4. Brush inside and out with a small amount of olive oil and place the potatoes back in the oven. Bake for 15 minutes, turning halfway through, until slightly crispy and golden brown.

5. While the potato skins are cooking, heat some oil in a frying pan and cook the chopped bacon and onions until the bacon is cooked and the onions are soft.

6. Take the potato skins out of the oven and, if you wish, spread a small amount of barbecue sauce on each of the potato skins.

7. Mix the reserved potato, cooked onions and bacon, and grated cheese in a bowl. Spoon the mixture evenly into the potato skins (don't worry if they're overflowing!) and bake in the oven for about 5 minutes until the cheese has melted.

Student Tip
Use a microwave to speed up the baking of the potatoes. (Read your appliance instructions for recommended cooking times.)

Spicy Chicken Wings

Spicy Chicken Wings

Leave these spicy wings marinating in the fridge all day until you're ready to eat!

You will need:
- 1 tsp crushed red pepper
- 2 tsp cajun seasoning
- 1 tsp chilli powder
- ½ tsp cornflour
- 6 tbsp brown sugar
- 100 ml (4 fl.oz) lemon juice
- 500 ml (17 fl.oz) orange juice
- 1 kg (2 lbs, 2 oz) chicken wings

Serves 4–6

1. First, make the marinade by combining all of the dry ingredients. Mix together well, then add the lemon juice and orange juice and stir.

2. Place the chicken wings in a deep bowl and cover with the spicy marinade. Cover and refrigerate for at least 6 hours.

3. Remove the wings from the marinade and place onto a baking tray. Return the marinade to a saucepan, and heat on a low setting until it has thickened.

4. Place the wings under a grill on a medium heat for about 20–25 minutes, turning occasionally and basting (covering) the wings with the sauce.

5. Serve with a fresh salad.

Student Tip
Serve the wings with chunky chips for a cheaper alternative to a take-away meal.

Garlic Bread

Garlic Bread

Great as a snack or as part of a main meal! This recipe is infinitely superior to pre-prepared garlic breads from the supermarket.

You will need:
- 3 large garlic cloves, peeled and finely chopped
- 100 g (4 oz) softened butter
- 2 tbsp flat-leaf parsley, finely chopped
- 1 ciabatta or 1 small baguette

Serves 2-4

1. Preheat the oven to 180°C / 350°F / gas mark 4.

2. Mix the garlic and butter in a large bowl and then stir in the parsley.

3. Cut the ciabatta or baguette in half and smear a large amount of the garlic butter on both slices.

4. Sandwich the two halves back together again. Then, wrap the garlic bread in foil.

5. Place the wrapped bread on a baking tray and put into a preheated oven to bake for 10 minutes.

6. Carefully unwrap the bread from the foil and open up. Serve while it's still hot!

Student Tip

Don't be seduced by discounted food stuffs you can't freeze. For example, salad may be reduced, but don't buy packet after packet as it won't last long!

Veggie Kebabs

Veggie Kebabs

These veggie kebabs are fantastic under a grill. Why not place them on a barbecue during the summer months?

You will need:
- 1 red onion
- 1 pepper, any colour
- 1 courgette
- 1 aubergine
- 6 cherry tomatoes
- 10 button mushrooms
- 2 tbsp olive oil

Serves 4

1. Preheat the grill to a medium heat.

2. Chop the onion, pepper, courgette and aubergine into thick slices. Leave the tomatoes and button mushrooms whole.

3. Push the vegetables onto skewers, alternating the different types for a varied selection.

4. Brush with a little olive oil and place under a hot grill until the vegetables have softened.

Student Tip
If you buy your fruit and veg at the supermarket, buy loose rather than pre-packed – it's cheaper.

Thai Fishcakes

Thai Fishcakes

The comforts of a fishcake coupled with the heat and flavours of Thai cuisine – it's hard to beat. A great way to impress your parents with your new-found cooking skills!

You will need:
- 340 g (12 oz) white fish fillets, skinned and cut into chunks
- ½ a beaten egg
- ½ tsp brown sugar
- 2 tbsp fresh chopped coriander
- ½ tbsp Thai red curry paste, available at most supermarkets
- ½ tbsp fish sauce
- ½ tsp salt
- 30 g (1 oz) green beans, finely chopped
- 2 tbsp olive oil
- Thai sweet chilli dipping sauce

Serves 4 as a starter

1. Check the fish thoroughly for bones, then place the fillets with all the ingredients, except the oil and dipping sauce, into a mixing bowl and stir until well mixed.

2. Divide and shape into four small cakes.

3. Heat the oil in a frying pan and cook the fishcakes gently for 4 minutes on each side.

4. Serve with a Thai sweet chilli dipping sauce and vegetables of your choice.

Student Tip
Fish is the ultimate brain food!
Tinned fish is good value, but also look out for special offers at the fresh fish counter.

Leek and Potato Soup

Leek and Potato Soup

This satisfying soup is quick, cheap and easy to make!

You will need:

- 1 tbsp oil
- 350 g (12 oz) potatoes, peeled and sliced
- 3 large leeks, washed and finely sliced
- 700 ml (1¼ pt) vegetable stock
- 300 ml (10 fl.oz) milk
- salt and pepper

Serves 6

1. First, heat the oil in a saucepan and fry the potato and leeks, until soft but not coloured.

2. Next, add the stock and cook until the potatoes are tender.

3. Add the mixture to a blender and process until smooth. Then, return to the saucepan and add the milk.

4. Season with salt and pepper and heat until hot. Then, pour into a bowl and enjoy.

Student Tip
You can make soup hours before you eat it. Just heat it up in a microwave or in a pan when you're ready.

Baked Bean Soup

Baked Bean Soup

You will need:

- 1 tbsp olive oil
- 1 large onion, chopped
- 1 large carrot, peeled and chopped
- 2 celery sticks, chopped
- 3 rashers of bacon, diced
- 400 g (14 oz) baked beans
- 330 ml (11 fl.oz) vegetable stock
- 330 ml (11 fl.oz) tomato juice
- 1 tbsp Worcestershire sauce
- ½ tsp paprika
- ½ tsp mixed herbs

Serves 4

1. Heat the olive oil in a large pan and gently fry the onion, carrot, celery, and bacon for 8–10 minutes.

2. Next, add the baked beans, vegetable stock and tomato juice, stirring continuously.

3. After 2 minutes, add a splash of Worcestershire sauce and the paprika and mixed herbs.

4. Cover the pan and simmer for a further 10 minutes or until the vegetables are tender.

5. Serve hot with fresh, crusty bread.

Student Tip

Always keep basic essentials like pasta, baked beans and tinned tomatoes in your cupboard. You can easily make a meal with them.

Main Meals

Home-made Burger

Home-made Burger

These fantastic burgers are easy to make. They freeze well and are so much better than the processed, ready-made ones you can buy.

You will need:
- 675 g (1½ lb) steak mince
- 1 onion, peeled and grated
- 3 tbsp finely chopped parsley and chives
- 1 tbsp Worcestershire sauce
- salt and pepper
- a pinch of cayenne pepper (optional) or, a dash of tomato sauce (optional)

Serves: 4–6

1. Place all of the ingredients into a large bowl, and, with clean hands, mix until completely combined.

2. Divide the mince into six portions, then mould into burger shapes by hand.

3. Chill the burgers in the fridge until you're ready to cook.

4. Preheat the grill and cook each side for 3–5 minutes until the burger is cooked to your preference. Place the burger in a bap, layer with cheese, salad or bacon, and enjoy!

Note: *The burgers can be frozen once shaped. Just defrost overnight in the fridge on a plate.*

Student Tip
Eat regular meals and don't eat too late
– it may be tempting to skip breakfast or dinner when you're in a rush, but you'll end up snacking later.

Baguette Pizza

Baguette Pizza

Wrap up these mouth-watering baguettes for a quick lunch on the go!

You will need:
- 1 tbsp oil
- 2 rashers of bacon
- 400 g (14 oz) tinned chopped tomatoes, or the same amount of fresh tomatoes, skinned and chopped
- 1 garlic clove, peeled and crushed
- 2 fresh basil leaves
- 2 baguettes or French bread
- 75 g (3 oz) cheddar cheese, grated

Serves: 4

1. Preheat the oven to 180°C / 350°F / gas mark 4.

2. Heat the oil in a frying pan and add the bacon. Fry for 5 minutes, turning halfway. Leave to cool, then chop the bacon into pieces.

3. Next, mix the tomatoes, garlic and basil together in a bowl. Then, gently heat in a saucepan.

4. Split the baguettes in half and spread the tomato mixture on the top.

5. Drizzle with a little olive oil, if desired, then sprinkle with grated cheese and the bacon bits.

6. Place on a baking tray and put the pizzas in the oven for about 10 minutes or until the cheese has melted and the bread is hot.

Student Tip
Experiment with toppings – use whatever spare or leftover ingredients that you have in the cupboard or fridge.

Pea and Pepper Risotto

Pea and Pepper Risotto

A great alternative to pasta, this dish makes a satisfying meat-free meal!

You will need:
- 1 tbsp olive oil
- 1 onion, chopped
- 1 garlic clove, peeled and crushed
- 1 red pepper, chopped
- 300 g (10 oz) risotto rice
- 600 ml (20 fl.oz) vegetable stock
- 200 g (7 oz) frozen peas
- a knob of butter
- Parmesan cheese, to serve (optional)

Serves 4

1. Heat the olive oil in a large saucepan. Add the onions and garlic and cook until the onions are soft.

2. Add the pepper and cook for another minute.

3. Add the rice and fry for about 1 minute, until the rice looks transparent.

4. Slowly add a small amount of the vegetable stock and stir well. Add the peas.

5. When the stock has been absorbed, add another small amount and stir well.

6. Keep adding more stock until the rice is soft. This will take about 15–20 minutes. Near the end, add the knob of butter to the pan. You may find you don't need to add all of the stock, or you may need to add a little bit more, depending on how dry the risotto rice is.

7. Serve with grated Parmesan cheese (optional).

Student Tip
Shop seasonally – you'll pay more for food that's been flown in from abroad, so save by buying your fruit and veg when it's in season.

Tuna Pasta Crispy Bake

Filling and delicious, your housemates will be jealous as you tuck into this great dish!

You will need:
- 600 g (1 lb, 5 oz) pasta
- 50 g (2 oz) butter
- 50 g (2 oz) plain flour
- 600 ml (20 fl.oz) milk
- 250 g (9 oz) cheddar cheese, grated
- 2 × 160 g tinned tuna, drained
- 100 g (4 oz) tinned sweetcorn, drained
- 75 g (3 oz) frozen peas
- 1 packet of ready salted crisps

Serves 6

1. Preheat the oven to 180°C / 350°F / gas mark 4.

2. Place the pasta in a saucepan of water and bring to the boil. Then, simmer for 12 minutes or until soft. Once cooked, drain.

3. Meanwhile, melt the butter in a saucepan and slowly stir in the flour. Heat for 1 minute, then stir in the milk gradually.

4. Remove the pan from the heat and stir in the cheese, leaving a handful for later.

5. Mix the pasta with the cheese sauce, the drained tuna, the drained sweetcorn and the peas. Place into a large baking dish and top with the rest of the cheese.

6. Crush the crisps and sprinkle on top.

7. Cook in the oven for about 15–20 minutes until the cheese is golden and starting to brown.

Student Tip
This meal can also be eaten cold!

Stir-fried Mixed Vegetables

Stir-fried Mixed Vegetables

An oriental twist on a basic veg stir-fry!

You will need:
- 1 tbsp oil
- 4 spring onions, cut into 2½ cm (1 in.) lengths
- 4 garlic cloves, crushed
- 2½ cm (1 in.) ginger, chopped
- 100 g (3½ oz) mange tout
- 100 g (3½ oz) baby corn
- 100 g (3½ oz) baby asparagus
- 1 red pepper, diced
- 1 courgette, sliced
- 2 tomatoes, skinned, deseeded and chopped
  or 400 g (14 oz) tinned chopped tomatoes
- 1 tbsp dark soy sauce
- black pepper

Serves 2

1. Heat the oil in a wok, and fry the spring onions, garlic and ginger on a high heat. Add the mange tout, baby corn, asparagus, pepper and courgette, and stir-fry for a minute or two.

2. Add the tomatoes and cook briskly to evaporate the excess liquid, then add the soy sauce, taste, season with the pepper and serve.

Note: *The ingredients listed are an example. Vary the vegetables depending on your taste, budget and what's available.*

Student Tip
Make this recipe go round a few more people by adding a drained tin of sweetcorn or haricot beans towards the end of cooking.

Irish Stew

Irish Stew

This is a simple, traditional and inexpensive stew that requires no frying or browning; it just goes straight into the oven – easy!

You will need:
- 900 g (2 lb) diced lamb or stewing beef
- 450 g (1 lb) potatoes, sliced
- 1 large onion, sliced
- 450 ml (16 fl.oz) beef stock or water
- a large sprig of fresh thyme
- salt and pepper

Serves 6

1. Arrange the meat, potatoes and onions in layers in a large, ovenproof casserole dish.

2. Pour in the stock, add the thyme and season with salt and pepper.

3. Cover and put in the oven on a low heat (150°C / 300°F / gas mark 2) for 2–3 hours.

Student Tip
This recipe can be adapted for other types of meat.
Keep your eyes peeled for good deals and
offers on chops or steaks.

Cottage Pie

Cottage Pie

Take a break from your books and cook up this great winter warmer.

You will need:
- 1 tbsp olive oil
- 450 g (1 lb) beef mince
- 1 red onion, chopped
- 120 g (4 oz) carrots, peeled and diced
- 2 tbsp plain flour
- 2 x 400 g (14 oz) tinned chopped tomatoes
- 1 tbsp tomato purée
- salt and pepper
- 50 g (2 oz) peas
- 675 g (1 lb, 7 oz) peeled potatoes
- knob of butter
- 60 ml (2 fl.oz) milk
- fresh parsely (optional)

Serves 4

1. Preheat the oven to 190°C / 375°F / gas mark 5.

2. Add the oil to a frying pan and cook the mince, onion and the carrots for about 10 minutes, stirring frequently. Once cooked, carefully drain any excess fat.

3. Stir in the flour, chopped tomatoes and tomato purée.

4. Add salt and pepper to the mixture, then add the peas. Cover and simmer for about 20 minutes, stirring occasionally. If the water evaporates too much, add more.

5. Meanwhile, cut the potatoes into small pieces and add to a saucepan full of water. Bring to the boil and then simmer for 15–20 minutes, or until the potatoes are soft. When cooked, drain.

6. Mash the potatoes with butter and a dash of milk. Season with salt and pepper.

7. Place the mince mixture into an ovenproof dish and cover evenly with the mashed potato. Bake in the oven for 20–25 minutes.

8. Serve with a garnish of fresh parsely, or a herb of your choice.

Student Tip
Make double the amount of cottage pie and freeze portions for later.

Sticky Chicken with Noodles

Sticky Chicken with Noodles

This dish will win your taste buds over!

You will need:

For the marinade:
- 4 chicken breasts, skinned
- 2 tbsp honey
- 2 tbsp light soy sauce
- 4 tsp grated fresh ginger
- salt and pepper

For the noodles:
- 2 tbsp olive oil
- ½ yellow, red and green pepper, deseeded and sliced
- 110 g (4 oz) mushrooms, sliced
- 1 red onion, sliced
- 2 spring onions, sliced
- 1 red chilli, deseeded and finely chopped
- 2.5 cm (1 in.) fresh ginger, peeled and grated
- 1 large garlic clove, peeled and crushed
- 250 g (9 oz) straight-to-wok medium egg noodles
- 2 tbsp light soy sauce
- 1 tsp honey
- salt and pepper
- a handful of fresh coriander, roughly chopped

Serves 4

1. Put the chicken breasts into a bowl. Cover with the honey, light soy sauce, ginger, and season. Leave to marinate for at least 30 minutes, up to 24 hours.

2. Heat half of the olive oil in a wok or frying pan and stir fry the sliced peppers, mushrooms, red onion and spring onion for 5 minutes. Remove to a plate.

3. Place the marinated chicken into a roasting tin lined with foil. Put under the grill and cook for 6 minutes on each side or until the chicken is firm and hot all the way through. Baste (cover) the chicken with the marinade as you cook.

4. Heat the rest of the olive oil in the wok and fry the red chilli, fresh ginger and garlic for one minute. Add the noodles and pour in the soy sauce and honey and cook for a further 2 minutes.

5. Return the vegetables to the wok and cook for one minute. Taste and season with salt and pepper.

6. Pile the vegetables and noodles onto four plates and serve the chicken on top. Sprinkle some fresh coriander over the dish to finish it off.

Student Tip
Healthy eating can be just as economical as tucking into a ready-meal!

Spaghetti Bolognese

Spaghetti Bolognese

Whip up this treat in a flash! Why not make double the bolognese and use it for a cottage pie or chilli?

You will need:
- 1 tbsp olive oil
- 1 large onion, finely chopped
- 4 or 5 garlic cloves, peeled and crushed
- 450 g (1 lb) minced beef
- 2 × 440 g (14 oz) tinned chopped tomatoes
- 3 tbsp tomato purée
- black pepper
- 450 g (1 lb) dried spaghetti

Serves 3–4

1. Heat the oil in a large saucepan, and on a medium heat, fry the onion and garlic until soft and translucent. Add the minced beef and brown well.

2. Stir in the chopped tomatoes and tomato purée. Bring to a simmer, and add the black pepper.

3. Simmer gently for an hour and a half, stirring now and then and adding a splash of water occasionally if it looks like it's drying out.

4. When the mince is well cooked and is soft with no chewy bits, cook the dried spaghetti (or the pasta of your choice) for 8–10 minutes in boiling, salted water, and serve with crusty French bread or the garlic bread from page 27.

Student Tip
Adding vegetables to mince makes it go further.
Try adding peppers, carrots and onions to the bolognese.

Spaghetti Carbonara

Spaghetti Carbonara

This is an Italian twist on our bacon and eggs, and it is easy to cook – as well as being delicious and cheap.

You will need:
- 1 tbsp olive oil
- 100 g (3½ oz) bacon, cut into small pieces
- 1 onion, finely chopped
- 1 garlic clove, peeled and crushed
- 100 g (3½ oz) mushrooms, sliced
- 450 g (1 lb) dried spaghetti
- 2 tbsp double cream
- 1 tbsp grated Parmesan cheese
- 2 eggs, beaten
- black pepper

Serves 3–4

1. Heat the oil in a large saucepan on a medium heat, and cook the bacon, onions, garlic and mushrooms, until the bacon is cooked and the mushrooms are soft. Meanwhile, cook the spaghetti for 8–10 minutes in a large pan of boiling, salted water.

2. Stir your cooked, drained spaghetti into the mixture over a low heat and stir.

3. Add the cream, Parmesan cheese and eggs to a measuring jug. Stir well. Pour into the spaghetti mixture and stir continuously until the eggs are cooked.

4. Taste and serve seasoned with black pepper.

Student Tip
Use a mixture of mature cheddar cheese and more expensive Parmesan cheese to lower costs.

Spicy Tuna with Penne Pasta

Spicy Tuna with Penne Pasta

This is great when you've got to cook for several people – delicious served hot or cold!

You will need:
- 100 g (3½ oz) dried penne pasta
- 1 onion, finely chopped
- 2 garlic cloves, peeled and crushed
- 1 tbsp olive oil
- 100 g (3½ oz) mushrooms, sliced
- 1 red pepper, diced
- 230 g (8 oz) tinned chopped tomatoes
- 200 g (7 oz) tinned tuna
- 2 generous splashes of chilli sauce
- black pepper

Serves 3–4

1. Cook the pasta according to the instructions on the packet, but turn off the heat 2 minutes before the pasta is cooked. Drain the pasta and set aside.

2. In a large pan, fry the onion and garlic in the oil over a medium heat until softened. Add the mushrooms and chopped pepper and stir-fry for about 5 minutes.

3. Add the tomatoes, and bring up to a gentle simmer, and cook until the sauce has thickened.

4. Add the tuna, chilli sauce and black pepper, and stir in. Cook for a couple of minutes.

5. Meanwhile, rinse your cooked pasta with boiling water. Add to the pan, stir, heat through, and serve.

Student Tip

Make a meal go further by adding pulses and beans. They will keep you full for longer and will bulk out your meals.

Chilli Con Carne

Chilli Con Carne

Easy to make, chilli con carne improves the longer it is cooked and is perfect when served with rice or jacket potatoes.

You will need:
- 1 tbsp oil
- 1 onion, finely chopped
- 5 or 6 garlic cloves, peeled and crushed
- 1 tsp ground cumin
- 1 tsp chilli powder
- 450 g (1 lb) beef mince
- 2 × 400 g (14 oz) tinned chopped tomatoes
- 3 tbsp tomato purée
- 1 red pepper, diced
- 1 green pepper, diced
- 4 or 5 green chillies, to taste
- 300 ml (½ pt) cold water
- 400 g (14 oz) tinned kidney beans, drained

Serves 6

1. Heat the oil in a large saucepan, and fry the onion and garlic over a medium heat until softened. Add the cumin and the chilli powder, stir and cook for a moment or two, then add the mince and brown it all over.

2. Add the tinned tomatoes and the tomato purée. Bring to a simmer and add the peppers, chillies and about 300 ml (½ pt) of cold water. Turn down the heat and simmer gently for at least an hour and a half until the mince is tender and has no chewy bits.

3. Add the kidney beans, and cook for another ten minutes.

4. Serve on its own or with rice or jacket potatoes and a side salad.

Student Tip

Without the chilli and kidney beans this recipe can be used as a meat sauce base for bolognese, lasagne and cottage pie.

Macaroni Cheese

Macaroni Cheese

Wholewheat pasta is a healthy alternative to regular white pasta. Give it a try!

You will need:

- 50 g (2 oz) butter
- 1 onion, finely chopped
- 150 g (6 oz) button mushrooms, cut in quarters
- 50 g (2 oz) fine wholewheat flour
- 1 tsp Dijon mustard
- 900 ml (30 fl.oz) milk
- 100 g (4 oz) cheddar cheese, grated
- salt and pepper
- 350 g (12 oz) wholewheat, short-cut macaroni
- 25 g (1 oz) freshly grated Parmesan cheese
- 2 tbsp fresh breadcrumbs

Serves 4

1. Heat the oven to 190°C / 375°F / gas mark 5. Melt the butter in a pan over a medium heat. Add the onion and mushrooms and cook for 5–6 minutes until soft. Sprinkle over the flour, and using a wooden spoon, mix over the heat for 1–2 minutes. Remove from the heat.

2. Add the Dijon mustard and then the milk, a little at a time, mixing well between additions. When all of the milk is incorporated, return the pan to the heat and bring to a gentle simmer, stirring all the time. Cook until the sauce is thick and creamy.

3. Mix in the cheddar cheese, season with salt and pepper, and remove from the heat.

4. Cook the macaroni in plenty of boiling, salted water. Drain and add to the cheese sauce. Pour the macaroni and sauce into an ovenproof dish, and sprinkle with the Parmesan cheese and breadcrumbs. Bake in the oven for 15–20 minutes until golden brown and bubbling.

Student Tip

Once you've perfected a recipe, tweak it slightly according to your personal taste and what ingredients you have lying around – you'll soon be on your way to creating your own meals from scratch.

Bangers and Mash

Bangers and Mash

Mmm, bangers and mash are the ultimate comfort food!

You will need:
- 450 g (1 lb) potatoes
- knob of butter
- 60 ml (2 fl.oz) milk
- 3 tbsp olive oil
- 8 good-quality sausages
- 4 onions, sliced (optional)
- 2–3 tbsp instant gravy granules
- fresh herb garnish (optional)

Serves 4

1. Peel and wash the potatoes. Next, boil the potatoes in a saucepan of water until they are soft (about 15–20 minutes).

2. Drain and mash the potatoes, adding the butter and milk until the mash is smooth.

3. Next, heat the oil in a frying pan and add the sausages and sliced onions. Fry until the sausages are brown and the onions are soft.

4. Add the gravy powder to a measuring jug. Pour in boiling water, then stir until the gravy thickens. Add more gravy granules if the sauce is too thin, or more water if it is too thick.

5. Serve the sausages and onions with the mash and pour the gravy over the top.

6. Garnish with fresh herbs, if desired.

Student Tip

Cheap cuts of meat are just as good for you, but when buying economy ranges of sausages, they are likely to contain far more rusk and fat than better quality versions. You will probably enjoy two good sausages more than four economy ones!

Easy Chicken Curry

Easy Chicken Curry

This chicken curry is so good you'll be dishing out seconds! Fantastic to share, or a meal for one, this recipe is sure to become a firm favourite!

You will need:

- 2 tbsp oil
- 1 onion, chopped
- 2 kg (4 lb, 4 oz) chicken breast fillets or thighs, cut into pieces
- 1 green pepper, chopped
- 3 tbsp balti curry paste
- 400 g (14 oz) tinned chopped tomatoes
- 250 ml (8 fl.oz) chicken stock
- 4 tsp cornflour
- 2 tbsp cold water

Serves 6

1. Preheat the oven to 180°C / 350°F / gas mark 4.

2. Heat the oil in a large saucepan and fry the onion and chicken pieces, until the onion is soft and the chicken is browned.

3. Next, add the pepper to the pan and fry gently, until softened.

4. Add the balti paste to the pan and stir, covering the chicken, pepper and onion. Then, pour the tomatoes and chicken stock into the pan.

5. Cover and cook in a preheated oven for 2–3 hours.

6. In the last 30 minutes of cooking time, combine the cornflour and cold water in a bowl, and then stir into the pan. Cover and cook for a further 15–20 minutes, or until the sauce has thickened.

7. Serve with pilau rice and naan bread.

Student Tip

Don't be afraid to improvise!
If you don't have an ingredient, use an alternative.
For example, plain yoghurt instead of cream in a curry.

Fish Pie

Fish Pie

The perfect dish for a student household. Fish can help boost brain power, it's low in fat and a good source of protein.

You will need:

For the mash:
- 375 g (13 oz) potatoes
- 50 g (2 oz) butter
- 60 ml (2 fl.oz) milk

For the filling:
- 25 g (1 oz) onions, finely chopped
- 1 tbsp flour
- 75 ml (2½ fl.oz) milk
- 60 ml (2 fl.oz) vegetable stock
- 150 g (5 oz) white fish fillets, diced
- 150 g (5 oz) salmon fillets, diced
- 1 tbsp chopped parsley
- 50 g (2 oz) cheddar cheese, grated
- salt and pepper

Serves 3

1. Preheat the oven to 180°C / 350°F / gas mark 4.

2. Peel and wash the potatoes. Next, boil them in a saucepan of water until they are soft (for about 15–20 minutes).

3. Drain and mash with a potato masher, adding half the butter and a splash of milk. Mash until smooth.

4. Next, make the filling – melt the remaining butter in a saucepan, add the onion and fry until softened. Add the flour and cook for 30 seconds, stirring.

5. Gradually stir in the milk and then the stock. Bring to the boil and cook for another minute.

6. Add the fish with the parsley. Simmer for about 3 minutes and stir in the cheese until melted. Season with a little salt and pepper.

7. Divide the filling between 3 ramekin dishes, or one large dish, and top with the mashed potato. Place into a preheated oven and cook for about 15 minutes or until the topping is golden and the filling is piping hot.

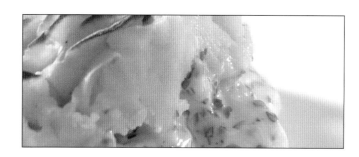

Student Tip
Use a tin of salmon rather than fresh fish for a cheaper alternative.

Sweet and Sour Chicken

Sweet and Sour Chicken

If you're strapped for time, this sweet and sour chicken dish is quick to put together.

You will need:
- 1 tbsp oil
- 4 chicken breasts, chopped
- 1 onion, sliced
- 150 g (5 oz) peppers, sliced
- 500 g (17½ oz) jar of sweet and sour sauce
- small tin of pineapple, drained and cut into chunks

Serves 4

1. Heat the oil in a frying pan and add the chicken and onion.

2. Cook on a high heat until the chicken has browned and the onions have softened.

3. Next, add the sliced peppers and cook for a further 2–3 minutes.

4. Pour over the sweet and sour sauce. Add the chopped pineapple and simmer for 4–5 minutes.

5. Serve hot with rice!

Student Tip
If you're in a shared kitchen, decide if you're buying your own food, or if it's cheaper to combine your resources and buy food that everyone in the house will share. If so, come up with a food kitty that everyone is happy with.

Chickpea Curry

Chickpea Curry

Chickpeas are a great student cooking ingredient. High in protein, they bulk out meals, fill you up and work well in curries.

You will need:

- 2 tbsp olive oil
- 2 onions, sliced
- 2 cloves garlic, peeled and crushed
- 1 tsp cumin powder
- 1 tsp coriander powder
- 1 tsp turmeric powder
- 5 cm (2 in.) piece root ginger, grated
- 3 green chillies, deseeded and chopped
- 400 g (14 oz) tinned chickpeas, drained
- 400 g (14 oz) tinned chopped tomatoes
- 1 tbsp mild curry paste
- pinch of garam masala

Serves 4

1. Heat the oil in a large frying pan and cook the onions and garlic until softened. Add the spices, ginger and chilli and cook for a further 30 seconds.

2. Next, stir in the chickpeas, chopped tomatoes and curry paste.

3. Cook for 1½ hours. Before serving, add the garam masala.

4. Serve the curry with pilau rice and naan bread.

Student Tip
It is cheaper to buy dried beans than tinned ones. Just soak them overnight, boil for 10 minutes then drain and simmer in fresh water for an hour until soft.

Toad in the Hole

Toad in the Hole

If your parents are coming to visit, make a fancier 'toad' by serving individual ones cooked in little, flat ovenproof dishes. Have two sausages per dish and cook for about 15–20 minutes. They can be served in their dish as well.

You will need:
- 100 g (4 oz) plain flour
- salt and pepper
- 3 large eggs, beaten
- 300 ml (½ pint) semi-skimmed milk
- 8 large good-quality sausages
- 4 tbsp vegetable or sunflower oil

Serves 4

1. Sift the flour, salt and pepper into a large bowl. Make a hole in the centre.

2. Put the beaten eggs into the hole and, working in a small circular motion, begin to incorporate the flour. When half of the flour is mixed in, begin to add a little of the milk.

3. All of the flour should be mixed in by the time half of the milk is added. Beat the resulting batter to make it smooth and lump free, then add the remaining milk.

4. Sieve the batter if it contains lumps and chill for 20–30 minutes.

5. Meanwhile, brown the sausages by frying them in a pan with a little of the oil. Preheat the oven to 220°C / 425°F / gas mark 7.

6. Heat the remaining oil in a shallow but large roasting tin in the oven. When almost smoking, place the sausages in at intervals and pour over the batter. Place in the oven and cook for at least 40 minutes, or until the batter is risen, brown and crisp. Do not open the oven for the first 20–25 minutes as the batter will not rise properly. Cut and serve with vegetables, such as broccoli or green beans, and gravy.

Student Tip
If you're craving some home-style cooking, the batter recipe can also be used to make Yorkshire puddings for a roast dinner.

Fajita Wraps

Spice things up with these chicken fajita wraps!

You will need:
For the salsa:
- 350 g (12 oz) fresh tomatoes
- ½ red onion, chopped
- 1 tbsp coriander, chopped
- 2 cloves garlic, peeled and crushed

For the filling:
- 2 tbsp olive oil
- 4 chicken breasts, cut into thin strips
- 2 tbsp fajita seasoning
- 1 red onion, chopped
- 2 garlic cloves, peeled and crushed
- 1 red pepper, deseeded and sliced
- 1 orange or yellow pepper, deseeded and sliced
- 8 soft flour tortillas

Makes 8

1. To make the salsa – chop the tomatoes into small pieces, making sure there are no seeds, and tip into a bowl.

2. Place the remaining salsa ingredients into the bowl and mix together well before transferring into a small serving bowl.

3. To make the fajitas – heat the oil in a large frying pan, and add the chicken strips. Brown the chicken and then sprinkle with the fajita seasoning.

4. Turn the heat down and add the onion and garlic. Cook gently for 5 minutes, and then add the peppers.

5. Put the flour tortillas onto a plate and cover with cling film. Next, put the tortillas into the microwave and heat for 30 seconds.

6. Remove the chicken and vegetables from the heat, pile into the warm tortillas, add the salsa and roll, tucking in the ends.

Student Tip
Save from the start – borrow kitchen utensils from friends and family!

Desserts

Apple Pie

Apple Pie

If you don't have the time to make your own pastry, buy pre-made shortcrust pastry.

You will need:
For the pastry:
- 240 g (8½ oz) plain flour
- 60 g (2 oz) caster sugar
- 150 g (5 oz) butter
- 1 egg

For the filling:
- 30 g (1 oz) butter
- 480 g (1 lb) peeled and chopped cooking apples
- 115 g (4 oz) caster sugar
- ½ tsp fresh grated nutmeg
- 1 pinch of cinnamon

Serves 6

To make the pastry:
1. In a large bowl, combine the flour and caster sugar using your fingertips.

2. Gently rub in the butter until the mixture resembles coarse breadcrumbs.

3. Make a well in the centre and break in the egg. Mix carefully to produce a firm but slightly crumbly pastry.

4. Cover with cling film and refrigerate for 20 minutes.

To make the filling:
1. In a saucepan melt the butter and then add the chopped apple. Cook on a low heat under a tight-fitting lid, stir occasionally and cook until soft. Add the sugar, then the nutmeg and cinnamon to taste. Cover and allow to cool completely.

2. When the pastry is rested, divide into two pieces. Cover a buttered, heatproof 20 cm (8 in.) pie dish with one half of the pastry rolled thinly. Press gently into the base and sides and trim off any overlapping edges.

3. Prick the pastry base with a fork to prevent it rising. Add the cooked, cooled apple to the centre of the dish and smooth out to the edges.

4. Roll out the remaining pastry, dampen the edges of the pie with a little water, then lay the pastry over the top of the pie dish and trim the edges. Decorate the pastry by pinching the edges between your finger and thumb and make a steam hole in the centre. Bake at 190°C / 360°F / gas mark 5 until the pastry is crisp and golden – approximately 25–30 minutes.

Student Tip
Baking is a great way to expand your recipe repertoire. Experiment with fillings – you could try sweet or savoury!

Bread and Butter Pudding

Bread and Butter Pudding

There's nothing like a bit of comfort food now and again. This pud tastes terrific and there's plenty to go round!

You will need:

For the custard:
- 135 g (4½ oz) eggs
- 60 g (2 oz) caster sugar
- a few drops of vanilla essence
- 550 ml (1 pt) milk

For the pudding:
- 10 slices white bread (slightly stale)
- 60 g (2 oz) butter
- 45 g (1½ oz) sultanas
- 30 g (1 oz) caster sugar
- 30 g (1 oz) apricot jam

Serves 4

To make the custard:

1. Whisk the eggs, sugar and vanilla essence together. Then, slowly add the milk, whisking all the time.

To make the pudding:

1. Lightly butter each bread slice, cut into triangles, then lay half of them in a buttered pie dish in a neat overlapping pattern. Sprinkle with sultanas.

2. Partly cover the layered bread slices with some of the custard.

3. Repeat with another layer of bread slices and sultanas, then cover with the rest of the custard mixture. Leave to stand so the custard soaks in. Sprinkle with caster sugar.

4. Wipe the edges of the dish and stand in a larger pie dish half filled with water. Bake at 175°C / 350°F / gas mark 4 for approximately 45 minutes–1 hour, or until the custard is set and the bread is golden and crusty.

5. When the pudding has cooled slightly, brush with apricot jam. Best served warm.

Student Tip
Don't let your old, stale bread go to waste.
Use it for this recipe instead.

Chocolate Fudge Brownies

Chocolate Fudge Brownies

A great pick-me-up during revision sessions!

You will need:
- 2 eggs
- 225 g (8 oz) caster sugar
- 100 g (4 oz) butter
- 3 tbsp cocoa powder
- 100 g (4 oz) self-raising flour
- 50 g (2 oz) pecans, chopped

For the fudge icing:
- 50 g (2 oz) butter
- 1 tbsp milk
- 100 g (4 oz) icing sugar
- 2 tbsp cocoa powder
- pecan or walnut halves, to decorate

Makes 15

1. Preheat the oven to 180°C / 350°F / gas mark 4.

2. Beat the eggs and the sugar together in a bowl, until light and fluffy.

3. Melt the butter in the microwave and beat in the cocoa powder before adding to the eggs and sugar. Sift the flour and fold into the main mix with the pecans.

4. Grease a 20 cm (8 in.) square cake tin with butter, then line it with baking paper. Pour in the mixture and bake in the oven for 40–45 minutes.

To make the fudge icing:

1. Melt the butter in a small pan and add the milk. Remove from the heat, then beat in the icing sugar and cocoa powder.

2. Spread icing over the cooked brownie and decorate with pecans or walnut halves. Cut into squares when the topping is firm.

Student Tip
Don't go shopping when you're hungry – you'll only fill the trolley up with unneccesary items.

Honey Flapjacks with Pecans and Almonds

Honey Flapjacks with Pecans and Almonds

These are great to grab on the way out in the morning when there's no time for breakfast!

You will need:
- 200 g (7 oz) butter
- 3 tbsp clear honey
- 200 g (7 oz) demerara sugar
- 285 g (9½ oz) jumbo rolled oats
- 100 g (4 oz) desiccated coconut
- 50 g (2 oz) flaked almonds
- 50 g (2 oz) pecans, lightly crushed

Makes 25–30

1. Preheat the oven to 180°C / 350°F / gas mark 4.

2. Gently heat the butter, honey and demerara sugar in a large saucepan until just melted.

3. Stir in the oats, coconut, flaked almonds and pecan nuts, and mix well.

4. Grease a 20 cm (8 in.) square baking tray with margarine, then pour in the mixture, spreading evenly. Bake in the oven for approximately 30 minutes.

5. Allow to cool in the tray for 10–12 minutes, then cut into squares with a sharp knife. Transfer the flapjacks to a wire rack to cool completely. Store in an airtight container.

Student Tip
Oats are a great source of fibre-rich nutrients and when mixed into this quick and easy flapjack recipe, they're the perfect treat.

Chocolate Pots

Chocolate Pots

Eat these heavenly chocolate pots before they melt!

You will need:
- 2 whole eggs
- 2 egg yolks
- 15 g (½ oz) caster sugar
- 1 tsp cornflour
- 570 ml (20 fl.oz) milk
- 100 g (4 oz) dark chocolate
- 4 tbsp chocolate and hazelnut spread
- 50 ml (2 fl.oz) whipped cream
- grated chocolate to decorate

Serves 6

1. Preheat the oven to 170°C / 335°F /gas mark 3.

2. Beat together the eggs, egg yolks, sugar and cornflour until well mixed.

3. Heat the milk until nearly boiling. Gradually pour the hot milk into the egg mixture whilst whisking.

4. Next, heat the chocolate and chocolate spread in a bowl over warm water. When the chocolate has melted, whisk into the egg mixture.

5. Grease six ramekins with a little butter and pour in the mixture. Cover the tops with foil and place in a roasting tray.

6. Fill the tray with water halfway up the dishes, and place in a preheated oven for 30–40 minutes or until the chocolate has set.

7. Remove the ramekin dishes from the tray and chill in the fridge until required. Decorate the tops with whipped cream and a little grated chocolate.

Student Tip
Make sure the kitchen is clean and tidy before you begin any cooking and always wash your hands before you start preparing a meal!

Smoothies

Hangover Cure

Hangover Cure

This smoothie will instantly make you feel more energised.

You will need:
- 350 ml (12 fl.oz) apple juice
- 3 handfuls apple, chopped*
- 3 handfuls celery, chopped
- 4 ice cubes, crushed
- a generous pinch of freshly grated root ginger

Serves 2

1. Place all of the ingredients in a blender and whizz until smooth.

2. Pour into two glasses.

3. Drink immediately.

* There's no need to peel the apples first. The apple peel adds to the fibre content of the drink.

Student Tip
If you have any leftover fruit that's about to go off, freeze it or chuck it all in a processor to make a healthy smoothie.

Beat the Winter Blues

Beat the Winter Blues

Packed full of vitamin C, this smoothie will help to stave off the dreaded freshers' flu!

You will need:

- 1 apple
- 1 carrot
- 350 ml (12 fl.oz) orange juice
- 4 ice cubes, crushed

Serves 2

1. Wash and quarter the apple, then wash and peel the carrot.

2. Place all of the ingredients in a blender and whizz until smooth.

3. Pour into two glasses.

4. Drink immediately.

Student Tip

Keep your immune system healthy and avoid 'freshers' flu' by eating plenty of oily fish, and fresh fruit and vegetables.

Brain Booster

Brain Booster

The exam season is looming – give yourself a brain booster with this heavenly smoothie.

You will need:
- 350 ml (12 fl.oz) orange juice
- 3 handfuls blueberries
- 1 small banana, sliced
- 4 ice cubes, crushed

Serves 2

1. Place all of the ingredients in a blender and whizz until smooth.

2. Pour into two glasses.

3. Drink immediately.

Student Tip
Blueberries are considered a 'super food' by nutritionists. It has been suggested that they can improve short term memory. Bananas provide slow releasing energy ... perfect for a long slog in an exam room!

Your Own Recipes